IT HAPPENED ON THE
MACKINAC BRIDGE

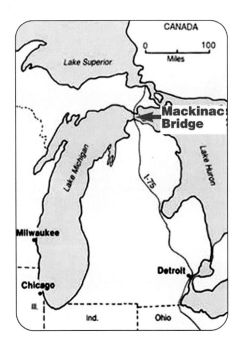

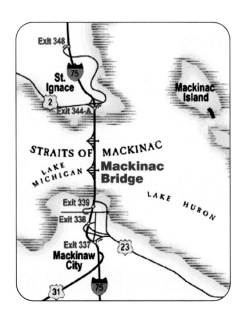

Is it Mackinaw or Mackinac?

Everything — from the Straits, to the island, to the bridge, to the town — that contains either Mackinac or Mackinaw, is pronounced with an "AW" sound at the end.

The Indian name for the area, Michinnimakinong, means "Land of the Great Turtle." When the French arrived in 1715, they spelled it Michilimackinac, but even though they spelled it with an "AC," they still pronounced it "AW."

The British arrived and took over the fort in 1761, and changed the spelling to an English ending of "AW," and the name was shortened to Mackinaw.

The French kept their "AC", and everything north of Mackinaw City still uses that spelling. Mackinaw City, Mackinaw Township and the U.S. Coast Guard cutter Mackinaw are amoung the references below the bridge that uses the "AW" ending. A Mackinaw coat, a Mackinaw boat and fresh Mackinaw whitefish are some others.

Regardless of the spelling, the pronunciation of "AC" is the same as "AW" — only the peninsulas that each spelling represents are different.

Confusion over the correct pronunciation of the bridge, island, straits, county, township, and city locations, in addition to objects that include whitefish, coats, and boats, due to different French and English spellings led to the author's description to settle the debate once and for all. (Author's collection.)

FRONT COVER (clockwise from top): Queen's Parade, 1958 (Courtesy of the Michigan Department of Transportation; see page 25), Mackinac Bridge Walk (Courtesy of the Michigan Department of Transportation; see page 94), Top of the Towers (Courtesy of the Michigan Department of Transportation; see page 125)

BACK COVER: Mackinac Bridge at night (Courtesy of the Mackinaw Area Tourist Bureau; see page 127)

IT HAPPENED ON THE
MACKINAC BRIDGE

Mike Fornes
Foreword by Lawrence Rubin

ARCADIA
PUBLISHING

Published by Arcadia Publishing
Charleston, South Carolina

Printed in the United States of America

Library of Congress Control Number: 2023952490

For all general information, please contact Arcadia Publishing:
Telephone 843-853-2070
Fax 843-853-0044
E-mail sales@arcadiapublishing.com

Visit us on the Internet at www.arcadiapublishing.com

This book is dedicated to the people who work to maintain and run the Mackinac Bridge 365 days per year. I salute you!

CONTENTS

FOREWORD

Mike Fornes has completed a monumental task in writing the history of the Mackinac Bridge since it opened in 1957.

Let me give you a clue: The operation, maintenance, and repair of the structure are divided into three eight-hour shifts. The key individual during each shift is the operations supervisor. His or her desk is positioned in the Brown-Fisher Administration Building so that he/she can observe the fare booths, the fare plaza, and down the center of the bridge as far as normal vision allows. This view of bridge traffic has been more recently augmented by the installation of video cameras mounted all the way across the bridge deck. One of the duties of the operations supervisors is to maintain three reports of occurrences during their shifts. Simple arithmetic tells us that during the first 50 years of bridge operations, there have been some 18,250 reports filed. Of course, many of the midnight-to-dawn shifts were routine. Nevertheless, Mike had to examine all of them. A formidable task!

In addition, his in-depth investigations of the accidents that occurred on the bridge in the past half-century have been most revealing in that the police reports and newspaper coverage provided far more additional information than the operations reports. I said, in 1985 when writing my own book about the bridge's construction years, that it was my intent to report in detail the events from 1950 to 1957 that led to the opening of the Mackinac Bridge. I added that history often depends upon the perch from which the observer reports the battle. Mike Fornes has picked up the task of reporting many years of happenings on the bridge from there and has documented a great story about a magnificent structure.

–Lawrence A. Rubin, executive secretary
Mackinac Bridge Authority, 1950–1984
April 2007

ACKNOWLEDGMENTS

Covering the Mackinac Bridge for radio, television, and newspaper is one of the most intriguing assignments I had among Northern Michigan news stories. It seemed that there was something different going on almost every day. It could be something funny that happened, an ironic or historic event, or those times of tragedy. It could be nothing happening at all on the days when the bridge simply provided a wonderful photography subject. No matter how many stories or reports I filed, gathering them all together was a task that was fun but also monumental. Larry Rubin, who had already written two books about the bridge at Mackinac, was my first source of motivation when he encouraged me to write about the bridge's happenings. No attempt is made here to rewrite his works or improve on their content. This book is merely an attempt to provide an update of what has happened on, over, and under this great bridge and feature the accounts of those who were there with pictures that helped to tell the story. A great resource was Susan Godzick and her staff at the wonderful Michigan Room of the Mackinaw Area Public Library. The people of the Mackinac Bridge Authority's staff are thanked for their willingness to help chase down dates and recall memories and circumstances, especially Walter North, Henry Lotozinski, Max Coburn, Bob Sweeney, Dean Steiner, and Lorraine Garries. They took a special interest in helping me organize people, places, and topics in the bridge's history. Other newspapers, besides my own *Cheboygan Daily Tribune*, assisted with permission to use photographs and story content. My grateful thanks go to the *Detroit News*, *Detroit Free Press*, *Grand Rapids Press*, *Lansing State Journal*, *Sault Evening News*, *St. Ignace News*, and the *Petoskey News/Review*. This book became a reality through the patience of composition editor Dan Pavwoski and graphic artists Charles Borowicz and Renee Glass. In addition, many local law enforcement personnel helped in significant ways, and I was lucky to have local resources nearby like photographer Greg Teysen, Terry Fitzpatrick, and Dick Campbell, who worked on the bridge as a diver, painter, maintenance man, and so much more during his years of employment there. The Michigan Department of Transportation is deserving of special thanks for its generosity in accessing archival photographs from a meticulously organized and maintained database, as were the visitors' bureaus in St. Ignace and Mackinaw City and the Mackinaw City Chamber of Commerce. It is my hope that readers will better appreciate all that went into past crossings and further marvel at David B. Steinman's genius during their next trip across.

Unless otherwise noted, all images appear courtesy of the Michigan Department of Transportation.

INTRODUCTION

In the days before there was a Mackinac Bridge, the only way to cross the five-mile Straits of Mackinac was by car ferry or train ferry. The *Chief Wawatam* and the *Sainte Marie* carried railroad cars and sometimes automobiles and passengers. The Michigan State Highway Department operated a ferry system between Mackinaw City and St. Ignace that took passengers and vehicles exclusively across the Straits of Mackinac. Ferry service began in 1923 in response to demand for service. By the last year of operation, the ferries transported just under 900,000 vehicles. Because lines of traffic sometimes backed up as much as 20 miles in either direction, for many the boat trip was an annual event to be endured over a period of 24 hours. For others, the entire process became a great adventure, especially for children of families who were on vacation. Just the sight of the ferryboats or at last seeing the Straits of Mackinac after enduring hours of waiting remains a treasured memory of many trips to the wilds of the north for fishing, camping, and sightseeing trips. The same trips take place today, but cross the Straits of Mackinac via the bridge that allows the same passage in less than 10 minutes. Citizens of Mackinaw City or St. Ignace now can use the bridge to commute to work or school or for recreation each day and sometimes have several crossings in a single day.

Prior to the bridge's opening in 1957, traffic line ups mostly occurred during holiday periods such as Memorial Day, the week surrounding the Fourth of July holiday, and sometimes the entire month of August and Labor Day weekend. Severe storms could also back up traffic until the boats began moving once again. But no time of year summarized the frustration of motorists crossing the Straits of Mackinac more than during firearm deer hunting season. At its peak in the 1950s, five boats were utilized on the route that had to be manned by full crews 24 hours per day. This meant rounding up the laid-off summer personnel and replacing those who would not or could not return. If a boat did not have a full crew, the United States Coast Guard did not permit it to leave the dock. Replacing a crew member was not simply a matter of recruiting a warm body. Each position was certified, and the individual employee had to have a certificate to fill the vacant position. There were approximately 325 employees on the five boats, and anywhere from four percent to six percent would simply disappear or call in sick. In addition, pursers and dock men had to be lined up along with office and warehouse personnel. In all, about 470 employees had to be pressed into service for peak season operations during hunting season. During the busiest period, which in those days began around November 11 and continued on until the morning of November 15, it is estimated that some 16 persons per day were recruited, hired, fired, promoted, and demoted. There was constant turmoil and change in getting people back to work for a short period after they had been laid off just two months before.

Without the employees, the boats could not operate. During the last deer season before the bridge, November 1956, there was a 23-mile line up of cars coming north that stretched 15 miles on US Route 27 and eight miles on US Route 31. Those who waited in traffic lines beyond the Mackinaw City limits will remember the adventures of heading off into the woods to answer nature's call. Some had nighttime encounters with skunks or porcupines that lurked nearby hoping to get fed by motorists who dumped trash and leftover food in the ditch. Many slept during the waits for movement as another boat loaded up, and kids sometimes had to awaken dad to get going again, or the cars behind would pass them up in the darkness.

The docks were a constant area of confrontation, if not combat. On the Mackinaw City side, 800 to 1,000 vehicles could be accommodated in the docking area. By the time hunters reached this point and had paid their fare to get on the ferry, they were no longer in the pleasant, jovial mood in which they began their trip. Many had been in line for six or seven hours already on the highway but now would have to wait another six or seven hours to clear the dock. Sometimes they would get the impression that the dockmaster was favoring one line over another and all hell would break loose. Yet even this alleged unfairness was child's play compared to their reaction if they thought some VIP was bucking the line. More than one car and its occupants nearly ended up in the Straits of Mackinac when irate hunters thought they were being cheated. Cars could not be left unattended on the docks or in the lines approaching the docks. Movement was frequent, if not constant, and an unattended car was quickly pushed onto the shoulder. Service stations were equipped with hoses to the gas pumps that were as long as 75 feet so that cars could be fueled while remaining in line as they passed the station. Besides the threat of running out of gas, filling the tank on the Lower Peninsula side was important because gasoline was considerably more expensive in the Upper Peninsula in those days. In an era before fast-food preparation and quick carry-out service, hunters were fair game for peddlers of smoked fish or pasties wrapped in newspaper. Sandwiches, cheese, crackers, and sundry edibles were brought out for sale, sometimes priced far above market value. Hawkers of souvenirs and trinkets took advantage of the hunters' early good nature and filled their pocketbooks from the northbound travelers. Occasionally, there were more severe incidents when hunters "lost" their wallets, and the ferry service was often on the receiving end of calls complaining about the shabby treatment of the travelers. Deer hunters, often the happiest people alive on their trip northbound, had to endure the return trip in the same long lines north and west of St. Ignace. By then, they were often bearded, tired, broke, and hungover, and many had no deer to show for their efforts.

The "Miracle Bridge at Mackinac" signifies joy and wonder to many—a landmark of the beginning of a great journey or perhaps a destination in itself. To others, the bridge can represent moments of unprecedented vistas, fear, anticipation, and wonder all at once. The Mackinac Bridge has seen comedy and sadness, glory and tragedy, life and death, and exhilaration and horror. It is a symbol of the state of Michigan and has encapsulated many aspects of life in the north country while enduring weather extremes, human nature, and the forces of mechanical engineering, routine maintenance, and added improvements. Day-to-day life on the bridge can range from the mundane to the newsworthy. This is the story of the normal, the unusual, the behind-the-scenes, and the most public moments "the Mighty Mac" has experienced since opening on November 1, 1957.

One

BEFORE THE BRIDGE TO

DEDICATION DAY

Years ago, there was no shortage of plans for linking Michigan's two peninsulas. A floating tunnel was suggested in 1920. At one point, a series of causeways and bridges were proposed to cross from Cheboygan to Bois Blanc Island, to Round Island, across the western tip of Mackinac Island, and then to St. Ignace. Financial and physical problems caused each of these plans to fail.

After World War II, G. Mennen Williams, a young Navy veteran, was nominated on the Democratic ticket for governor and promised to revive the Mackinac Bridge project if elected. He was chosen governor in November 1948 and began collaborating with Sen. Prentiss M. Brown of St. Ignace to secure financing and the logistics of getting the bridge built. Democrats and Republicans in the legislature joined to establish the Mackinac Bridge Authority, and in 1951, the authority reported to the legislature that a bridge at the Straits of Mackinac was feasible from all standpoints—engineering, financial, and economic.

Dr. David B. Steinman, at 63 years old, was named as consulting engineer for the Mackinac project in 1953. After much political haggling, the Mackinac Bridge Authority explored the idea of selling bonds to finance the bridge rather than rely on taxes or other public funding. Due to the bond market being "soft" at the time, the authority sought assurance of state support in the form of an indenture clause of $417,000 to pay for maintenance in the event the bond payments were not met. The sale of the bonds was arranged; however, the bridge was almost stopped when Michigan senator Haskell L. Nichols filed a lawsuit in the Michigan Supreme Court asking for an injunction to prevent approval of the bond sale by the Michigan State Administrative Board. The lawsuit was filed 24 hours before the scheduled sale of the bonds. Had this move succeeded, the $417,000 appropriation would have lapsed, and the bridge would have been set back at least a year and possibly for many years. The court refused the injunction and upheld the state administrative board's approval of the bridge's financing. The bonds were sold, and the bridge project was approved at a cost of $96,400,033.33.

In the days when the Michigan Department of Transportation's car ferries supplied the connection between the state's two peninsulas, traffic routinely backed up at the docks in Mackinaw City (above) and St. Ignace. The wait could be many hours long, depending on the season of the year. It was not uncommon to see long lines heading into each town, with cars pulled off to the side of the road waiting to get to the docks.

The State of Michigan had invested heavily in ferryboats, docks, and employees to facilitate the crossing between Mackinaw City and St. Ignace. As the crowds grew over the years between 1923 and 1954, bigger car ferries joined the fleet and traversed the Straits of Mackinac. At one time, several ships worked the route named for various cities in the area, including the *City of Petoskey* (right), the *City of Cheboygan*, and the *City of Munising* (below), along with one named the *Straits of Mackinac*. Eventually, the largest car ferry of all went into service: the *Vacationland*. A double-ender that could load and unload 150 vehicles from either end, the ship worked the period of highest passage in the 1950s until the Mackinac Bridge was built.

Michigan governor G. Mennen "Soapy" Williams (left) ran for governor on the promise that if elected he would champion the cause of getting the Mackinac Bridge built. Williams, a Democrat, partnered with Sen. Prentiss M. Brown of St. Ignace (below), also a Democrat, to forge a bipartisan effort in the Michigan legislature to gain support for the project. The pair worked tirelessly and overcame many obstacles to get the bridge built on time, on budget, and at no cost to Michigan taxpayers. (Left, courtesy of Bentley Historical Library, University of Michigan.)

Local interest in building a bridge at Mackinac included the owner of Mackinac Island's Grand Hotel, W. Stewart Woodfill. His influence and persuasion convinced many that the construction of the bridge would open the Upper Peninsula to tourism, industry, and commerce. Woodfill had the foresight to realize that the bridge would include benefits to Mackinac Island, even though no vehicles could travel there due to the island's ban on automobiles.

A veritable genius, David Steinman mastered double-digit multiplication in his head while in the second grade. He grew up selling newspapers in the shadow of the Brooklyn Bridge and later recalled telling fellow newsboys that someday he was going to build bridges like the famous structure that towered above them. They laughed at him. He earned his doctoral degree in engineering at the age of 19 from Columbia University and was awarded honorary doctoral degrees from 22 other universities. He was hired as the bridge's architectural engineer from the top three in the world who were interviewed. Steinman proved that he knew how to build bridges, as his firm was involved in the construction of more than 400 bridges on five continents throughout the world.

Dr. David B. Steinman designed the Mackinac Bridge foundations to cooperate with the forces of nature, not resist them. His design plan was to support the superstructure and any live load it would carry by a safety factor of four. The steel superstructure, in turn, would withstand wind pressure of 50 pounds per square foot, or wind velocities up to 600 miles per hour. The highest wind velocity recorded to date in the 1950s at the Straits of Mackinac was 78 miles per hour. Years later, the highest wind speed yet recorded occurred at 4:08 p.m. on May 9, 2003, and lasted about one minute. There was no time to close the bridge. The anemometer read 124 miles per hour. Steinman was paid $3.5 million for bridge engineering fees and hired a staff of 350 engineers to solve the design problems he faced in building the Mackinac Bridge. They produced more than 85,000 blueprints that accounted for nearly five million rivets, 931 tons of concrete, and 42,000 miles of suspension cable. All this was accomplished using slide rules and logarithms—no computers in those days.

At a bond sale conducted by the New York firm of the Union Securities Corporation, the Mackinac Bridge Authority received the proceeds of $96,400,033.33 in bond sales to build the bridge on February 17, 1954. Prentiss M. Brown, known as the "father" of the Mackinac Bridge, was asked how he wanted the funds and decided that a certified cashier's check would do just fine. Now contracts could be issued to American Bridge, United States Steel, and other contractors to get the project underway. The bonds were retired in 1986.

An artist's concept of the Mackinac Bridge showed how the underwater portion of the span would be built, with two giant caissons driven more than 100 feet through the bottom of the lake into bedrock. The caissons, resting in 210 feet of water, would support two towers—552 feet tall above the waterline—above which the cables would be strung to hold the span in place. Two-thirds of the bridge structure is underwater and invisible to the naked eye. Dr. Steinman's dream was becoming a reality that had long been envisioned by the people of Michigan.

Groundbreaking ceremonies were held in St. Ignace on May 7, 1954, and in Mackinaw City on May 8, with surveyors' towers built on shore. Large crowds attended the festivities on both sides of the Straits of Mackinac. Construction began immediately, and although the work on the water shut down each winter, it continued on the mainland with crews readying bridge sections that were brought out by barge in the spring and summer to be lifted into place. The bridge was completed on time, on budget, and with private financing through the sale of bonds. The ferryboats were charging an average of $3.40 per car and passengers when the boats stopped running on November 1, 1957.

Construction began in the spring of 1954, in St. Ignace, Alpena, and Ambridge, Pennsylvania, among other locations. At Ambridge, the giant tower sections were laid flat on the ground and assembled first for exact fitting, then disassembled for transport to the construction site in Northern Michigan. Railroads and barges were used to bring various preconstructed materials to the Straits Area.

The caisson sections, looking like huge "donuts," were constructed in Alpena and floated to the bridge site with the help of cranes and barges. Fitted together one on top of another, the bottom section had a beveled cutting edge that penetrated the lake bed as more and more weight was added, with additional sections welded into place. Eventually, it cut into bedrock where it was permanently set to support the towers.

By May 1957, the Mackinac Bridge was nearing completion. The "sidewalk superintendents" studied daily progress through shoreside telescopes and their own camera lenses. Only the center span—perhaps the most difficult stage of the bridge's construction—had yet to be completed. With a target opening date of November 1, crews rushed to finish construction and paved the final roadway sections mere days before the first traffic crossed. Years later, people who saw this photograph were sure they were in it, although no faces are visible. Automobiles and people looked the same in that era, and many tourists recalled being at this spot watching the construction process. (Courtesy of the Ken Teysen family.)

Larry Rubin, the first executive secretary of the Mackinac Bridge Authority, was tasked with planning the bridge's opening day ceremony—on November 1, 1957—traditionally not a good bet for decent weather to accommodate an expected crowd of 5,000 outdoors in Northern Michigan. Reasoning that a brief opening ceremony on that date would be better followed by a full-fledged dedication ceremony in late June, Rubin planned two gatherings to cover the expected November gales and snows.

November 1, 1957, dawned as an overcast, foggy day, and the overnight rain had stopped well short of the opening ceremony's start time. Overcoats and men's hats were standard fare, but no one looked uncomfortable in above-average temperatures. The headline in the newspaper read, "Michigan Is One," appropriately describing the mood of the state that day.

Vehicles lined up days in advance at Mackinaw City to be the first to cross the new Mackinac Bridge. Anticipation was high at the ferry docks too, as customers filled the *Vacationland* on its last trips to St. Ignace and back to Mackinaw City. Passengers received commemorative tickets as souvenirs of the journey. Soon, traffic was turned away at the docks, and motorists were told to line up at the bridge as the ferries were no more.

Governor Williams and his wife, Nancy, rode in the convertible limousine with Prentiss M. Brown in the seat behind them as Larry Rubin drove. The parade of dignitaries stopped at the center span for photographs and heard the roar of the crowd gathered ahead at St. Ignace, who saw them approaching and knew the bridge was soon to open. With 150 newspapers represented and three television networks standing by with film cameras, the governor was ready to take the wheel for the trip through the tollbooth to pay the first fare—a historic moment sure to be seen across the country if not the world. Nancy Williams stopped her husband from driving, as he had not renewed his driver's license; he was used to being chauffeured.

As the motorcade approached the tollbooth, the crowd could wait no longer and surged forward to greet the dignitaries. Nancy Williams was at the wheel, saving her husband any possible embarrassment from critics who may have learned of his expired license. Governors are usually chauffeured to official events, and apparently the renewal had slipped Governor Williams's mind.

Governor Williams then walked to the tollbooth and presented a large cardboard check for $3.25 to represent the first fare to be paid. Prentiss M. Brown doffed a toll collector's cap and accepted the check on behalf of the Mackinac Bridge Authority, posing for a perfect photo opportunity. A Michigan state trooper radioed to a colleague on the Mackinaw City side to start the traffic—the Mackinac Bridge was now open.

Northbound traffic streamed across the bridge and lined up at the tollbooths, but the wait was nothing compared to what had been endured during the days of the ferryboat crossings. The cost was similar to what had been paid to cross in the boats, and many employees from the ferry system were hired on to work in various capacities for the Mackinac Bridge Authority.

Motorists were handed commemorative cards by Boy Scouts signifying that they had crossed the bridge on the first day of travel. Many locals in St. Ignace and Mackinaw City still have their souvenir tickets from the last day of ferry travel and the first day of crossing the bridge. The mementos have been handed down through generations as remembrances of one of the biggest days in the histories of their small towns.

Southbound traffic came to Mackinaw City that day on the new four-lane highway that was the Mackinac Bridge. Interstate 75 had not yet been built, and US Routes 27 and 31 were the main highways of the day, taking motorists to Cheboygan, Petoskey, and other points south. Houses had been moved from this location and streets divided to build the bridge, and in three years' time, Mackinaw City had taken on a very different look. Some businessmen were sure no one would ever stop in town now that the bridge approach would carry them past the downtown area.

The next big days in the Straits Area came on the weekend of June 26–28, 1958, when Larry Rubin's bridge dedication was to take place. The events followed a full week of celebrations in Sault Ste. Marie, Petoskey, Cheboygan, Mackinac Island, St. Ignace, and Mackinaw City. The weather was absolutely perfect when two sections of green ribbon were tied together, stretching from Mackinaw City to St. Ignace, celebrating that Michigan's two peninsulas were now united by the bridge.

A parade of Michigan county and festival queens followed, riding in white convertibles donated by Oldsmobile for the occasion. Cloudless blue skies prevailed with flat-calm seas and windless conditions accenting a perfect thermometer reading in the mid-70s. The weather could not have been better, and the idea of postponing the dedication from the previous November 1 seemed like pure genius, despite the unseasonably warm and dry conditions that day.

The parade route began in St. Ignace and crossed the bridge to Mackinaw City, routing through each town's main streets. Miss Mackinaw City was Diane Krueger, one of 83 queens who rode in the parade. Most Michigan counties were represented, along with festival queens from various communities throughout the state. Usually, the girl's father drove her in the parade, with her mother riding along as a guest in the front seat. The queens' families had the car for the week to go to the various events they were required to attend.

Lenore Allen represented her hometown as Miss St. Ignace, the gateway to the Upper Peninsula. The queens attended many celebratory dinners and other festivities the week of the dedication, and the bridge parade was the final event planned for them. Thousands of people crowded into the small communities on either side of the bridge to take part in many activities scheduled for that week.

Mrs. Michigan, Barbara Dolan of Greenville, was also honored in the parade of queens. Following the parade, crowds headed for the state dock where the ferries no longer ran, and Larry Rubin had organized a trade fair for the many businesses that wanted to be a part of the celebration. Souvenirs, treats, and gifts bearing company names and images of the Mackinac Bridge were handed out to the crowds until straight-line winds of 60 miles per hour suddenly entered the region. Sheets of rain forced people to run for their cars, parked blocks away, as Mother Nature reminded all of her power. The Mackinac Bridge stood unharmed.

The three top bridge engineers in the world, David Steinman, Othmar H. Amman, and Glenn B. Woodruff, were brought to St. Ignace for an interview with the Mackinac Bridge Authority and were asked, "Gentlemen, what would happen to one of your foundations if a boat loaded with ore crashed into it?" Only David B. Steinman answered: "In my case, the boat would sink with a serious loss of life." Steinman got the job over Amman and Woodruff. Amman had built the George Washington and Whitestone Bridges in New York and many others throughout the country while Woodruff had participated in the design of several structures, including the Oakland Bay Bridge. Steinman later wrote the words below about the Mackinac Bridge inside his 1958 Christmas card. (Courtesy of the Mackinaw Area Public Library.)

The Song of the Bridge

The light gleams on my strands and bars
In glory when the sun goes down.
I spread a net to hold the stars
And wear the sunset as my crown.

Dr. and Mrs. D. B. Steinman

Christmas, 1958

Two

MICHIGAN'S ICON

Once the Mackinac Bridge was completed, it did not take long before businesses in the Straits Area, in Michigan, and throughout America began to realize that the new five-mile bridge was something special. It had displaced San Francisco's Golden Gate Bridge as the longest suspension-span bridge in the world. But beyond its length, the miracle bridge at Mackinac had united an entire state, joining the Upper and Lower Peninsulas in a way that evoked great pride from both ends of Michigan. This bridge stood for Michigan and began to show up in advertisements and on billboards and designs that promoted the state. It became a featured picture on postcards and souvenirs of every description. From the dedication day of the bridge onward, it was apparent that Michigan's new engineering feat was being recognized as practically the eighth wonder of the world.

The postmaster general of the United States, Arthur Summerfield, came to the Straits of Mackinac to take part in the Mackinac Bridge Dedication Festival ceremonies. Summerfield was met by more than 300 people at the Pellston Airport and continued to Mackinaw City where he broke ground there for a new post office, spoke at St. Ignace, then gave an address on Mackinac Island where he was the guest of honor at a Grand Hotel luncheon. Summerfield's presence was due to the issuance of a 3¢ Mackinac Bridge stamp that went on sale on June 25, 1958. The stamp was used to pay for first-class letter-sized mail sent anywhere in the United States. Both the Mackinaw City and St. Ignace post offices participated in special day-of-issue sales, sending hundreds of thousands of pieces of pre-addressed mail on its way to collectors and dealers bearing the postmark "Mackinac Bridge," dated June 25. A commemorative 14¢ stamp was issued in 2010.

Mackinac Bridge souvenirs began selling the year the bridge opened, 1957. Many varieties hit the shelves in area gift shops, including T-shirts, pens, hats, sweatshirts, and more. This tray and souvenir plate set date back to the bridge's dedication weekend in June 1958. It seemed as though any item found in a gift shop was now offered with the image of the bridge or simply the name of the bridge. Shot glasses, decks of cards, wallets, coin purses, pillows, candles, stained glass, puzzles, and figurines all depicted Michigan's new icon. (Both, author's collection.)

If one purchased at least 10 gallons of gasoline at Leonard gas stations after the bridge opened, one could get a souvenir Mackinac Bridge frosted beverage glass. The promotion was very popular with vacationing tourists who hoped to complete a set during their travels through Michigan. It seemed as though all companies and businesses wanted to find a way to use the bridge in their advertising campaigns and somehow identify themselves with the bridge. Consumers today continue to purchase clothing, gifts, and items with the bridge as a theme. (Author's collection.)

Great Lakes Splendor

The State of Michigan has used the bridge to promote tourism and self-image in many ways, including vehicle license plates. "Great Lakes Splendor," "Spectacular Peninsulas," and "Mackinac Bridge" editions adorn the license plates of citizens looking for an individual touch to match the color scheme of their vehicles or to suit individual tastes. Some people combine the bridge plates with vanity names or words to provide a very personalized look to their vehicles. (Both, courtesy of the Michigan Secretary of State.)

The "Mackinac Bridge" edition of the Michigan license plate was celebrated with a photo opportunity at the top of a Mackinac Bridge tower. Michigan secretary of state Ruth Johnson (left) and Mackinac Bridge Authority chairman William H. Gnodtke (right) posed with the newest of the state's license plate designs. Johnson held the popular "Pure Michigan" edition that also made its debut in 2012.

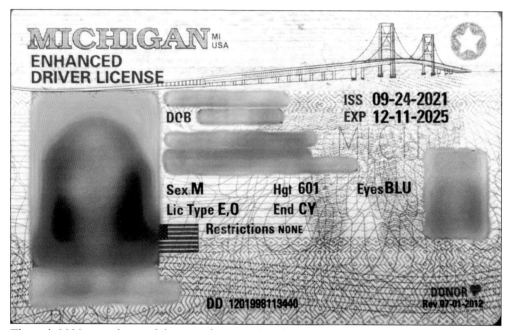

Through 2023, every licensed driver in the state of Michigan carried a photograph of the Mackinac Bridge in their pocket, wallet, or purse. The state's licenses varied in design for underage drivers, those with commercial or enhanced licenses, and for state identification cards, but all had the Mighty Mac as part of their imagery until 2024, when the Michigan Department of Transportation (MDOT) introduced a new look that featured the state's seal. (Author's collection.)

The Mackinac Bridge has used its lighting capabilities over the years to proclaim milestone anniversaries and events. In 1976, bridge workers created a giant "76" design to observe America's bicentennial celebration. The lights stayed lit the entire year. In 1987, a similar lighting array celebrated Michigan's sesquicentennial celebration with a large "150" visible from miles away.

In 2007, the Mackinac Bridge Authority celebrated the bridge's 50th birthday with a yearlong series of events, culminating with a week of festivities in late June. A giant birthday cake was the centerpiece of a dinner in St. Ignace. Reunions were held for ironworkers who built the bridge and administrative, maintenance, and toll collection staff. Media coverage was extensive, and traffic was heavy crossing the bridge as motorists wanted to be a part of the 50-year party.

A series of posters were created and sold as commemorative souvenirs; some hung as banners from downtown streetlight poles in Mackinaw City and St. Ignace. The state had developed an enthusiasm for bridge history and memorabilia that was reminiscent of the atmosphere surrounding the bridge's dedication in June 1958 after its November 1 opening in 1957.

After numerous attempts failed to create a Mackinac Bridge postage stamp in time for the 50th anniversary in 2007, a 14¢ stamp was eventually issued in February 2010. Representatives of the Mackinac Bridge Authority joined United States Postal Service officials in displaying the new stamp on Pier 22, the bridge's north anchor pier (above). On Memorial Day weekend 2017, a giant American flag was hoisted above the roadway at the bridge's north tower. A permanent compartment was later built on the tower to hold the flag so that it can be displayed on other occasions to honor Americans.

The Mackinac Bridge provides a perfect backdrop for a Great Lakes phenomenon, "blue ice," that forms during many winters along the shoreline at Mackinaw City. Crowds throng to the Straits Area to see and photograph nature's artistry during typically cold, sunny afternoons in mid-to-late February when the winds and currents pile up huge chunks of ice along the shoreline. The ice appears blue due to a lack of air bubbles and the way the eye perceives the ice, allowing the light to be undisturbed as it passes through the giant shards. (Above, courtesy of MLive.com; below, courtesy of Greg Teysen.)

Often photographed, the Mackinac Bridge can take on many different moods that vary with sunlight, moonlight, seasons, weather conditions, and angles. Seeing it from different directions can give completely different perspectives to the appearance of the bridge. Water conditions in the Straits of Mackinac also change frequently and cause the bridge to take on different looks when the lakes are flat calm or churned up in a tempest. Whether it is seen in peaceful, serene conditions or in the middle of a winter storm, the bridge has many personalities. The bridge's image has been used in countless advertisements, promotions, and logos in the state of Michigan and beyond. The Mackinac Bridge truly stands for Michigan. (Courtesy of the Mackinaw Area Visitors Bureau.)

Three

MILESTONE CROSSINGS

Among the many successful and routine crossings on the Mackinac Bridge, some very unusual events have taken place. Famous people have crossed. Marriages have been proposed, and marriage ceremonies performed. New lives have begun. Sadly, deaths have occurred as well. The birth of a child can take on a stressful tone when the event occurs on the Mackinac Bridge. It has happened three times, and two involved premature babies born in ambulances en route to the hospital. Another baby was born in a car while crossing the bridge.

Despite the usual fares, what must the toll collectors have wondered the day they saw a scene out of the Old West approaching? Roland Church, his wife, and their two daughters rode in a Conestoga wagon hitched to two horses at 5:00 a.m. on June 30, 1973, escorted by a bridge patrol officer. Regarding the toll, they probably charged by the axle, as they normally do.

Over the years, there have been some notable bridge accidents that ranged from fender benders to crashes of a serious nature that produced fatalities and made them newsworthy.

One of the strangest accidents ever to occur at Mackinac took place in the 1960s when a boat hit a car. The boat blew off the top of a car, struck another car in the opposite lane, and fell into the Straits of Mackinac. Eight boats were blown off car tops in 1974 alone, and in 1973, lost boats were reported 10 times. There were 11 in 1976. Residents along both peninsula shorelines are used to finding life jackets, coolers, caps, and canoes on area beaches from vehicles that did not have these items secured in the backs of pickup trucks or inside boats being trailered across. The year 1976 also saw 300 bales of hay spilled onto the bridge deck when a farmer's load became loose.

Better than 99.9 percent of the vehicles that pass through the toll gates at Mackinac have a successful, uneventful crossing. Over the years, the Mackinac Bridge Authority has kept a diligent count of the number of crossings recorded each day, each month, and each year. When another million milestone crossing is reached, it is always a special event to be celebrated.

FIRST CAR ACROSS BRIDGE

The car that was the first fare-paying vehicle to cross the bridge was on display for some time near the tollbooths before it was eventually relocated to a Grand Rapids museum. The owner, a jazz band drummer from Chicago named Al Carter who made a hobby of being first at various events, at one point wanted to sink it off the bridge's center span, but environmentalists blocked the plan.

The fall deer hunting season has always been part of crossing the Straits of Mackinac, as hunters who head to the Upper Peninsula returned by car ferry with their trophies. When the bridge opened on November 1, 1957, hunting season opened just two weeks later, and it was just a matter of time until the first successful deer hunter arrived at the tollbooths. When it happened, the bridge crew was ready with a commemorative plaque. The hunter's car was then led across the bridge and stopped briefly for a photograph to document the occasion. The toll collectors usually keep a running count of deer brought across the bridge and update the totals to reflect whether the count is up or down from the previous year.

Once the cold weather set in, it took a while for motorists to adjust their speed to icy and snowy conditions while driving on the new bridge. The bridge's first-ever traffic fatality happened on July 22, 1966, when Russell McKeighan, 56 years old, of Highland Park, Michigan, remarked to his companion what a lovely view of the area they were enjoying, heading northbound near the center of the span. He then slumped over, quick as that, dead of a heart attack. Over the years, there have been traffic fatalities on the Mackinac Bridge, but far fewer than most any other five-mile stretch of Interstate 75. Most have involved attempted U-turns, distracted driving, and too much speed for current conditions.

Celebrities have been welcomed at the Mackinac Bridge for decades, and the first of note would have to be John F. Kennedy, who was running for president in 1960 and paid a visit to the bridge to campaign for votes. Gov. G. Mennen Williams welcomed Kennedy and posed for a picture on the bridge. Kennedy went on to win Michigan and won the presidency. Over the years, Lady Bird Johnson and Pres. George H.W. Bush have visited the bridge, as have television stars that include *Dirty Jobs* star Mike Rowe; *Bonanza's* Dan Blocker, who played the character Hoss; and Ann B. Davis, who was Alice from *The Brady Bunch*.

As time went on, calculations showed that soon the one-millionth vehicle would be crossing the Mackinac Bridge. Although it was certain to be a momentous occasion, very little took place in the way of fanfare. As a Volkswagen approached and was identified as the one-millionth crossing, a passenger stood and waved to bridge personnel through the vehicle's sunroof. The event was captured in an historic photograph.

The two-millionth crossing was more of an important event. A vacationing family was greeted by Michigan governor G. Mennen Williams and Mackinac Bridge personnel. A sign was prepared to place on the windshield of the car for purposes of the photograph for posterity.

The three-millionth crossing was greeted by Mackinac Bridge Authority executive secretary Larry Rubin, who started the practice of presenting the honorees with a framed picture of the bridge. Two men were in the vehicle and looked as surprised as anyone that they had been selected as a milestone crossing.

When the five-millionth crossing occurred, the father and son in the family were delighted at the fuss being made over their good fortune. The mother did not seem as enamored, however, but the sign was apparently moved across the windshield to allow her to see and to be in the photograph.

Mackinac Bridge representatives are pictured here closing in on the 150-millionth vehicle to cross the bridge, driven by Richard Snyder of Clare, Michigan. The Mackinac Bridge Authority uses an electronic counting procedure to keep track of vehicle crossings. "We would know when we had 500 vehicles to go, 100 to go and so on, then we'd close down to one lane and identify the vehicle as it came through," said former bridge administrator Walter North.

On June 16, 2022, Kurt Dalman was driving with his wife, Anna, and their children Seth and Teresa. The Dalmans were presented with a framed print of the Mackinac Bridge to commemorate their vehicle being the 200-millionth to cross the bridge. They also received a local gift basket filled with all kinds of goodies. (Courtesy of the Mackinaw City Chamber of Commerce.)

During the 2007 celebration of the Mackinac Bridge's first 50 years, plans were made to replicate the original parade of queens in convertibles that crossed the bridge during the dedication in 1958. Unlike Oldsmobile's iconic fleet of white convertibles, an array of vehicles was assembled to transport various dignitaries in the parade. All were convertibles though, and the group assembled with a truckload of media reporters leading the way to photograph and record the event. This view is from midway up one of the bridge towers.

Chevrolet Corvettes were not the only cars used in the 2007 parade of queens and dignitaries who crossed the bridge during the span's 50th anniversary celebration. Some were classic cars and others muscle cars built for speed, but all were convertibles and all were shined up and looking their best. Among the notables riding in the parade and waving for the cameras were two Michigan governors, Jennifer Granholm and William Milliken.

It can be a dirty job to scrape and paint the lowest spot inside the Mackinac Bridge towers, so naturally that was one of the tasks assigned to Mike Rowe of the Discovery Channel's television show *Dirty Jobs*. Rowe visited the bridge in 2007 to record an episode of his program and also climbed a cable all the way to the top of a tower—a journey he nearly did not complete. While at the Straits of Mackinac, Rowe accepted an offer to take on another dirty job on Mackinac Island and cleaned horse manure from the island's streets.

Another way to cross the Straits of Mackinac is to swim the five-mile distance *next* to the bridge, not under it. Swimming events have taken place on Labor Day during the Mackinac Bridge Walk and during the Mackinac Bridge Swim, held in July. Most entrants wear wet suits and tow inflatable buoys behind them, carrying hydration and snacks. The event raises money for various charitable causes and is conducted under the supervision of the United States Coast Guard. The route begins at Colonial Michilimackinac in Mackinaw City and concludes at Bridgeview Park in St. Ignace.

There was a lot of excitement at the tollbooth in 2013 when NASCAR's Brad Keselowski drove his No. 2 Miller Lite Ford Fusion across the Mackinac Bridge. Keselowski, from Rochester Hills, Michigan, competes full-time in the NASCAR Cup Series. He was the 2010 NASCAR Nationwide Series champion and the 2012 NASCAR Sprint Cup Series champion and has had several other wins since then. In addition to driving, Keselowski is also an entrepreneur and owns his racing team, RFK Racing.

October 24, 2018, was an important date for social media contest winners Emily Misner and Cord Wilson, who won a trip to the top of the Mackinac Bridge tower. The prize is an experience enjoyed by very few, as only those nonprofit organizations who submit applications have a chance at raffling off a tower tour for a lucky winner. In this case, Wilson used the magnificent view and breathtaking height to propose to Misner while atop the tower. She accepted. Over the years, proposals and weddings have taken place during the Mackinac Bridge Walk and on the bridge.

Four

TOLLBOOTH TALES

As long as it costs money to cross the Mackinac Bridge, there will always be a need for toll collectors. Motorists say the darndest things at the tollbooths and ask questions that may have to be heard to be believed. There are questions about the remoteness of the area:

"Are there any restaurants up here?"

"Do you need to see my passport?"

"Is this still Michigan, or did we cross over?"

"If I go up and around, will I end up over there?"

Then, there are questions about the lakes:

"Which lake do they get the smoked fish from?"

"Are we on the island now?"

"How are Lake Huron and Lake Michigan connected?"

There are also questions about paying the toll:

"Can you break a $10 bill?"

"Is the Upper Peninsula lane cheaper?"

"This is the first time I've been up here since they put in the tollbooths."

The tollbooths have always been here. And then there are questions or comments from those who try to get out of paying the fare altogether:

"I just got on in Mackinaw City. Is it still $4?"

"You have to pay both ways now?"

"I remember when the toll was only 75¢."

"We're with a Girl Scout troop. Do we still have to pay?"

Of course, the bridge toll has never been less than $1.50 and has always been charged in both directions. Sometimes people crossing the bridge test local knowledge about the obvious:

"Which direction does US Route 2 West go?"

"Which one is Exit 344A?"

"Where do I pick up Interstate 75?"

Motorists are already on Interstate 75. Some get personal with the toll collectors:

"What's up, bridge lady?"

"Hey baby, why don't you just hop in and head south with me?"

"Look kids—a real Indian!"

And sometimes they get ridiculous:

"Is there a net under the bridge?"

"What are the life rings for?"

"Have you seen an SUV hauling a boat?"

"What time does the bridge swing over to Mackinac Island?"

Through it all, the staff of the Mackinac Bridge Authority handles the constant dialogue with grace and dignity.

1.50	MOTORCYCLE
8.00	BUS
14.00	TRUCK COMBINATION MORE THAN 5 AXLES
12.00	TRUCK COMBINATION 5 AXLES
11.00	TRUCK COMBINATION 4 AXLES
10.00	TRUCK COMBINATION 3 AXLES
8.00	3 AXLE TRUCK SINGLE UNIT
7.00	2 AXLE TRUCK W/6 TIRES
4.25	2 AXLE TRUCK W/4 TIRES
8.00	CAR WITH 2 AXLE TRAILER OR COACH
5.75	CAR WITH 1 AXLE TRAILER OR COACH
3.25	CAR

When the Mackinac Bridge opened in 1957, the tolls were very similar to what motorists paid to use the ferryboats. After increases to $3.50 and $3.75 in the next two years saw the number of crossings continue to decrease; the tolls were then dropped to $1.50, and commuters as well as vacationers began using the bridge. The lesser fare likely helped open the Upper Peninsula and stayed in effect for decades. Tolls were eventually increased in 2003 to $2.50 for a passenger car and $3 per axle for commercial motor coaches and went to $4 for automobiles and $5 per axle for commercial vehicles in 2012.

The tollbooths were constructed so that more or less lanes could be opened from either direction, depending on traffic loads. Unlike some bridges, the Mackinac Bridge has always charged the same fare in both directions, rather than a higher fare one way. It was thought that this policy encouraged crossings to the Upper Peninsula, rather than charging a higher one-way fare to get there. More traffic crosses northbound than southbound.

In the early years of operation, the Mackinac Bridge Authority provided bus service to pedestrians needing to cross, especially those working on one side or the other. The practice was discontinued when numbers decreased and patrol officers began transporting pedestrians. Eventually, maintenance workers took up the task and continue the work today.

Motorists often comment to toll collectors about conditions on the bridge, be it wind, snow, or heavy traffic. However, one day someone asked a toll collector if he knew there was a deer at mid-span, and it was certainly a surprise. Sure enough, a deer was 2.5 miles out onto the bridge, and many motorists had passed without mentioning it at the tollbooth. Bridge administrator Walter North helped walk the deer back to Mackinaw City.

After giving locals a break on fares by offering books of scrip tickets, it was realized that too much cost was going into printing more books of tickets. Tokens were tried next in 2002, commemorating the various car ferries that preceded the bridge. One challenge to the token system was that the collection baskets would fill with snow in the winter and jam up with ice. In 2003, a merchant was caught buying tokens and reselling them for a profit that still saved their customers money to cross the bridge. Debit account cards were then offered and evolved into the Mac Pass stickers for windshields. Credit and debit cards were not accepted until 2017. When the token lanes and machines to accept them and fare cards were implemented, some collectors feared it meant the eventual end of their jobs. However, many locals who use the alternative payment methods use the automatic lanes when in a hurry but pass through manned toll collector lanes just to say hello or request or pass along information.

Despite the many conveniences offered to customers for paying tolls on the bridge, about 30 people each year attempt to avoid paying the bridge toll, costing the Mackinac Bridge Authority less than $200 annually. In 2001, a Jackson, Michigan, man flipped a hockey puck to the toll collector instead of paying a $1.50 fare. When apprehended by police, he was found to be carrying drugs and a concealed weapon, went to jail, lost his car, and paid nearly $3,000 in fines and costs. Skipping through the tollbooth today without paying at the Mackinac Bridge means a maximum $500 fine and 30 days in jail due to a bill signed in 2005 by Michigan governor Jennifer Granholm. (Author's collection.)

Another duty of toll collectors is to sometimes be on the lookout for a particular car or driver because of a request by the police. Sometimes it is due to a call from a family. As an example, in 1979, the Mackinac Bridge Authority delivered 212 emergency messages to motorists via the toll collectors. For years, the Salvation Army would help out people who had no money to cross and appeared to need more help than just the bridge toll. In recent times, fare collectors have offered cashless motorists directions on how to find the closest ATM at a local bank. In 2007, fares became restricted to either all American or all Canadian currency—no mixing. In 2023, the rule changed to American currency only.

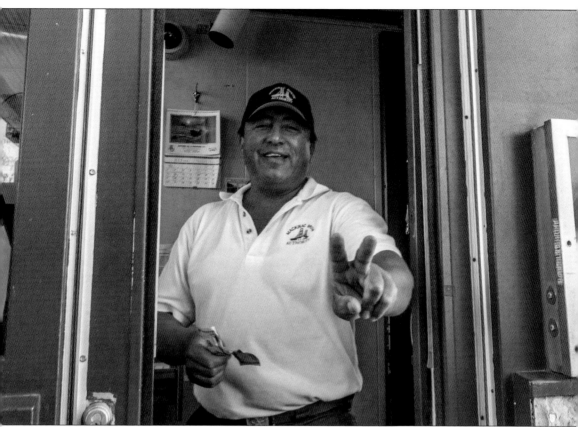

Some travelers who have come a long way seem to want someone to talk to, and view the tollbooths as a sort of rest stop or break from the highway miles. There are convenient rest areas on both sides of the highway adjacent to the tollbooths for this purpose, but some drivers just seem to want to chat. Perhaps it is the idea that most travelers who cross the five-mile span have just completed a drive of considerable distance, whether they are arriving from the north or the south. Add to that the fact that many who cross the bridge are doing so for the first time and are likely quite unfamiliar with the Straits of Mackinac area or Northern Michigan in general. Very few motorists found a more friendly and humorous conversationalist than toll collector Pat Rickley.

Toll collectors have the first eyes on Mackinac Bridge weather conditions, which can change rapidly. They are another layer of protection for the weather instruments at the center span and inside the command center at the St. Ignace side of the bridge. Besides weather radar and temperature gauges, wind speeds are recorded as far away as the White Shoal Lighthouse, 15 miles to the west, giving a heads-up to approaching weather conditions. Monitors in the operations center display and record all toll transactions from each lane, allowing supervisors to see the type of vehicle that is passing through and how much they are being charged. Toll collectors can easily report situations to a supervisor, who can then answer questions or relay concerns to the St. Ignace Post of the Michigan State Police, located across the street for easy access to the bridge and Interstate 75 or US Route 2 to the north and west.

Five

MAINTENANCE AND OPERATIONS

The maintenance of the Mackinac Bridge involves work of all types. There is painting, electrical, steel and iron repair, welding, and cement work done on the bridge itself and plowing, sanding, washing, and occasional patching of the roadway on the bridge. Contractors come in to do the heavy-duty painting, paving, and electrical jobs, but much work of that sort is also performed by the local crew that staffs the Mackinac Bridge Authority's maintenance department.

Every summer, some portion of the bridge undergoes a sandblasting and painting process that has been a never-ending job since 1958. Weather permitting, the Mighty Mac is paintable if it is warmer than 40 degrees with low humidity and wind velocities are within safety margins to have workmen on the bridge. It takes seven summers to paint the entire bridge, and when they finish, the painters start all over again. During inclement weather, the Mackinac Bridge Authority's paint crew will sometimes paint the inside of the two giant towers—an extremely difficult and uncomfortable duty. There is also a total of 6,800 feet of guardrail that has to be sandblasted, primed, and given three coats of paint. The north and south approach viaducts also require spot blasting, priming, and finish coating.

Maintenance workers do not salt the bridge in the winter; instead, they apply a sand and gravel mix for traction. When it gets plowed into the lake, it is going right back to where it came from in the first place—the bottom of the lake.

The operations department of the Mackinac Bridge is really the pulse and nerve center of the bridge. It is in the Brown-Fisher Administration Building's front offices that day-to-day decisions are made, hourly assessments figured, emergency measures taken, and judgments decided to sometimes close the bridge for short periods of time. The operations department moves vehicles, people, and events across the span and coordinates this traffic—averaging 12,000 vehicles per day—around scheduled maintenance, weather, and emergency conditions. Although the main goal of operations is to keep the bridge open and running smoothly, dealing with closings is part of its job.

When the Mackinac Bridge first opened in 1957, the temperatures were too cold to paint it until the next spring, so the structure kept the "red lead" coating it had first undergone to prevent winter rust and corrosion. The Mackinac Bridge Authority adopted the green and cream colors after a company inquired as to what the bridge would look like when completed for a color advertisement it wanted to place in a magazine. The authority had not yet decided on a color scheme but liked the picture used in the advertisement so much they decided the colors were perfect.

The bridge flexes to accommodate weather stress or vehicle weight. There are two large finger joints at the towers to accommodate all the expansion of the suspended spans. There are 11 smaller finger joints and five sliding joints across the Mackinac Bridge. In addition, there are 13 expansion joints for the south viaduct spans, with one for each of these simple spans. This adds up to 31 total joints. All suspension bridges are designed to move to accommodate wind, changes in temperature, and weight. It is possible that the deck at the center span could move as much as 35 feet (east or west) due to high winds, but it has never come close to that.

This type of movement would only happen under severe wind conditions. The deck would not swing, or "sway," but rather inch slowly in one direction based on the force and direction of the wind. After the wind subsides, the weight of the vehicles crossing would slowly move it back into the center position. This could take days. At times, it appears that the suspended portion in the middle has "blown out" and looks somewhat flexed to one side, usually to the east due to prevailing northwesterly winds.

Part of Dr. Steinman's bridge design called for two grated lanes in the middle of the suspended span. Although motorists often remark that they would prefer to drive on the outer lanes, the grated lanes are lighter in weight than the paved lanes and allow air to flow through, providing less resistance to wind flow. In addition, water can drip through to eliminate standing water on the highway. Plows can push snow down through the grates or over the side, and since the bridge is sanded—not salted—the sand goes right back to where it came from in the first place, the bottom of the lake. The grating has been replaced as needed over the years and has in recent times been cut up and sold as souvenirs.

The suspension cables are the key to building a bridge like the one at the Straits of Mackinac. The individual cables are about the size of a No. 2 lead pencil and were banded together during construction. They were then hydraulically compressed into a single column and encased in a pipe measuring 24.25 inches in diameter. These main cables support the side stay cables that actually hold up the suspended bridge structure. Maintenance is performed on the cables, they are painted like the rest of the bridge, and lights are mounted throughout their length. Workmen must climb the cables to paint and inspect them, change the light bulbs and the colored globes, and get from one location on the cables to another. There is no other way to do it.

The Mackinac Bridge towers are 552 feet tall above the waterline, and each stands in 210 feet of water. The caisson base that supports each tower is anchored more than 100 feet into the bottom of the lake into bedrock. Each tower has an elevator in each side that can carry a couple of passengers from lake level all the way to the top at a very slow speed of about 100 feet per minute. Entry to the towers is via a submarine-type hatch that is difficult to enter to access the elevator, as *Dirty Jobs* host Mike Rowe (above) was about to find out. At the top level, after climbing over a series of crisscrossed girders, the last stretch is 30 feet straight up a vertical steel-rung ladder to another hatch that puts the climber on the top deck of the tower. Karen Southway (below), Miss Michigan/America 1961, made the trip during a statewide tour. Atop the towers are several communications antennae that take advantage of the height of the towers.

The towers are rarely painted, utilizing a creeper that raises and lowers painters up the sides of the tower. The creepers are specialized equipment that makes painting such a tall structure practical and also provides safety for the painters. The interiors are painted too, to prevent rust, but this work is usually only performed on bad weather days and is a low-priority job.

The unique "reach-all" truck allows a giant arm to extend over the side of the bridge and provide a stable platform for painting or maintenance work. The apparatus can be controlled from up on the roadbed, affording a solid base to counter the load over the side.

Gone are the days when painters were lifted up the cables in 55-gallon drums. Advances in safety equipment and OSHA regulations now provide safer equipment and conditions that are better for the workers and the environment. A movable platform under the suspended span allows painters and maintenance workers a stable workspace while under the bridge and affords them a good look at the underside of the structure to inspect for anything that does not belong there.

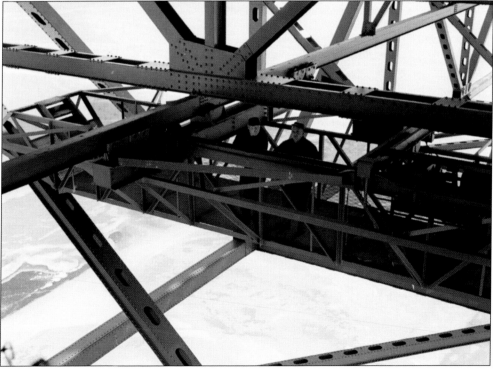

In another era without OSHA regulations and EPA, DEQ, and EGLE controls, painting the bridge was done in a very different manner than it is today. Even the paint was different. Today, sandblasting and painting are done under a canvas tent that keeps all contaminants contained. A giant vacuum is operated from the bridge's road deck to draw paint chips, toxic fumes, and excess paint spray into a tanker truck parked above. The bare metal is inspected for signs of wear or rust and treated. Then, a newer, safer, zinc-oxide paint mix is applied with a spraying system that does a faster, more complete job than the old brush-and-can method; it is still used today where needed. (Author's collection.)

In the 1980s, for example, it was estimated that it took 40,000 gallons of the old lead-based paint and eight summers to finish the bridge from one end to the other. Then the paint crew would start over again. Today, the process takes about a year less with the zinc-oxide formula. (Author's collection.)

After a long winter of plowing snow and sanding the bridge deck, spring clean-up involves plowing all the sand and gravel from the roadway and blowing the surface free of stones or winter debris that could make travel unsafe. After inspection, it is then time to begin resurfacing areas that need new asphalt. Although the orange barrels do slow down traffic flow while this work is being done, holiday weekends and days of expected heavy travel are avoided. Weather can also play a role in when the work takes place.

The bridge can be lit in several different color combinations, notably all amber lights during the Halloween and Thanksgiving seasons; red, blue, and green at Christmastime; and patriotic red, white, and blue during the summer for Independence Day. A new twist added in April 2013 saw all cable lights in blue for Autism Awareness Month. The design proved to be very popular with travelers. The partnership of the Mackinac Bridge Authority and the Autistic Children's Treatment Network brought the "Light It Blue" campaign to the Straits Area.

Six

CROSSING UNDER AND OVER

Since the bridge is 200 feet above the water at its highest point mid-span, it has become an obstacle for some people who cannot bear the thought of driving across. In the first year of operation, the Mackinac Bridge Authority transported at least six jittery motorists across the five-mile span. In each instance, the drivers were afraid to make the crossing on their own and appealed for assistance. In five cases that first year, the owners were content to surrender the wheel and make the trip while sitting alongside the driver. In another, however, the driver not only requested help, but also begged not to be driven over in his own vehicle.

Bridge patrol officers say that more men than women ask for help and that the shakes are worse at night than during the daytime.

The Motorist Assistance Program is for "timid" drivers and provides a driver to get the vehicle to the other side. Cars, trucks, motorcycles, RVs, and even semitrailers have been driven across for frightened owners. By 1977, the number requesting help had risen to around 200 people annually, and by 1987, it reached 400. It continued to increase, and more than 1,300 motorists ask for a driver each year these days, the Mackinac Bridge Authority reports.

In 1977, a total of 82 cars ran out of gas while crossing the bridge. Bridge patrol vehicles carry gasoline onboard to help in these situations. By the year 2000, the number had grown to more than 360 cars per year—or an average of almost one per day.

Extra-wide and extra-long loads are escorted across the bridge, as are placarded loads carrying explosive, corrosive, and hazardous materials. High-profile vehicles are escorted at slow speeds when winds are high.

An unusual escort took place in 1987 when a man attempted to walk across the bridge carrying a large wooden cross. Eventually, he was convinced to accept a ride.

Countless ships have passed below the bridge and aircraft above it—some too close.

The Mighty Mac would be endangered daily by trucks transporting explosives, acids, and nuclear materials were it not for the escort crews. Mackinac Bridge Authority escort drivers do the job every day safely, silently, and with the care that is needed to protect the bridge and its travelers. Dangerous loads such as radioactive material, explosives, and overwide and overweight vehicles must be accompanied by the bridge patrol. Escort drivers also lead high-profile vehicles across when the winds are high. The caravan moves at 20 miles per hour with flashers on and does not pass any other vehicle. Trucks carrying gasoline and propane do not require special permits from the State Police Fire Marshall's Division in order to travel on Michigan highways. Others, considered "placarded loads," have a metal sign that indicates the nature of their permit. Those trucks must wait for an escort before crossing the bridge. (Author's collection.)

Many "timid drivers" are regulars, well-known to the escort personnel. Timid southbound drivers can ask for an escort at the tollbooth, while northbound drivers can call from a courtesy phone or their own cell phone. Patrol officers or maintenance workers drive vehicles across for those who cannot handle it. Those who grab the driver are the hardest to handle, bridge personnel say. They try to keep them talking and tell them to look straight ahead at the roadway, not off to the sides. One motorist-assist sent the escort driver to a van, where the female driver was visibly shaking with fear at the prospect of crossing the bridge. Nothing the driver said could calm the woman, who was unable to secure her seat belt due to her shaky hands. "Just about then I looked in the back of the van and it was full of cages with snakes inside—big ones," the escort driver recalled. "I asked if any of the snakes were poisonous, and she said they all were. And this lady was scared to drive across the bridge?" (Author's collection.)

In 1959, the Royal Yacht *Brittania* sailed under the bridge with Her Royal Majesty Queen Elizabeth II. The ship was accompanied by a destroyer escort that followed to provide security. "The Queen came out on deck and saluted the bridge as they crossed under," said Larry Rubin, bridge administrator at the time. "We stopped traffic as the Brittania approached and crossed under. People on the bridge honked their horns for her. It was quite the thing."

The Greek freighter *Castalia* rammed into the bridge's north tower in 1968 in dense fog, tearing out a chunk of concrete below the waterline 23 feet wide and 15 feet high. The incident did not affect bridge operations or traffic on the span. Damage is seen here above the waterline of the bridge's north tower. Diver Dick Campbell is preparing to inspect the tower's underwater caisson, where more damage was apparent. The concrete was patched and tested, showing the tower to remain strong.

The tall ship *Pride of Baltimore*, under full sail, passes under the Mackinac Bridge in foggy conditions. The Straits of Mackinac can be a very foggy place, especially in the months of May and June when rapidly warming air develops with the onset of summer and mixes with water that is still cold from a winter of being frozen solid. Fog can develop during other seasons too, when the reverse effect is taking place in the fall and when water is trying to freeze in the winter. June 25, 1958, the day before the bridge's gala dedication was to begin, the German motor vessel *Korbeck* collided with the SS *New York News* in dense fog. No one was injured, and the damage to each vessel was slight. (Courtesy of the Mackinaw Area Visitors Bureau.)

At times, the fog can be so thick that only the tops of the towers are visible, while conditions are clear on land. Three Marine Corps Reserve officers died on September 10, 1978, when their private plane, flying in dense fog from Mackinac Island, crashed into one of 180 pairs of vertical two-inch-thick steel suspender cables hung from the main cable structure to hold up the bridge deck. The point of impact was about 80 feet above the roadway and 120 feet south of the north tower. There was no damage to the bridge, which sheared off the wings of the single-engine Cessna 182 as it passed through 40-foot gaps between the suspender cables. The victims were identified as Maj. Virgil Osborne, 35 years old, and Capt. Wayne Wisbrock, 32—both of St. Louis, Missouri—and Capt. James Robbins, 31, of Neosho, Missouri. (Courtesy of the Mackinaw Area Visitors Bureau)

On April 24, 1959, Capt. John Lappo flew a giant United States Air Force bomber under the suspension span of the Mackinac Bridge at high speed. Lappo, a 39-year-old reconnaissance aircraft commander at the time, was in command of a six-engine B-47E Stratojet returning to Lockbourne Air Force Base near Columbus, Ohio, from England. Wanting to show his crew the new Mackinac Bridge, he told his crew, "Hang on—we're going under that bridge."

The crewmen, used to Captain Lappo's daring nature, likely knew he could pull it off. One member, a young navigator, was not so sure. At an altitude of 75 feet, Lappo had less than 100 feet of clearance beneath the underside of the bridge. The navigator mentioned the stunt that night to his father, an Air Force general. Lappo pleaded guilty in a military court to flying closer than the 500-foot limit over water when not landing and lost his privilege to fly. Today, a pilot would face Federal Aviation Administration sanctions if caught flying too close to the bridge. (Courtesy of the United States Air Force.)

When it comes to commercial shipping seen on the Straits of Mackinac, there are two distinct categories of vessels that route courses under the Mackinac Bridge. There are "lakers" and there are "salties." A "laker" (pictured) is a ship that stays within the Great Lakes, usually carrying iron ore, taconite pellets, finished steel, or limestone to ports on Lake Michigan, Lake Huron, or Lake Superior. They begin passages early in the spring as soon as the Soo Locks open and usually work through the "gales of November" until winter lay-up time, depending on schedules and the ultimate closing of the locks. A "salty" is a ship that comes through the St. Lawrence Seaway to bring cargo to Midwest ports, often staying to work within the lakes for the summer to "earn their keep" before eventually leaving in the fall with a load of grain or wheat, bound for an ocean voyage to a foreign destination. (Courtesy of the Mackinaw Area Visitors Bureau.)

Seven

WALKING AND PARADING THE MIGHTY MAC

Over the years, hundreds of thousands of people have walked across the bridge on Labor Day, but the event had a humble beginning. In 1958, the International Walkers Association proposed a walking race across the bridge to be held during the June dedication festivities. The Mackinac Bridge Authority granted the request for an organized walking effort, and on June 25, history was made when 60 people showed up from the International Walkers Association to walk across. Larry Rubin championed the idea of making the bridge walk an annual event, and in 1959, the second bridge walk was held, this time on Labor Day. About 250 racers and pleasure walkers combined to cross, with the date changed from late June to the end of summer to try and promote vacation travel to lengthen the tourist season through the end of August. The races were sanctioned by the Michigan Amateur Athletic Union in 1960, and the turnout doubled to 500 people. Soon, casually walking the bridge with family and friends became more popular than racewalking across. The numbers increased to 1,500 in 1961 and 2,500 in 1962, to 4,000 in 1963, then 20,000 in 1970, and an all-time high of 85,000 when Pres. George H.W. Bush walked in 1992.

Over the years, many different types of groups have arranged with the Mackinac Bridge Authority to cross as a group. The St. Ignace Antique Auto Show, held each June, has for many years provided a colorful bridge crossing that has featured old cars, hot rods, retro cars, and classic cars. Bicycle tours enjoyed the crossing for many years, as have parades of Harley Davidson motorcycles, tractors, MINI Coopers, Ford Mustangs, ATVs, Jeeps, Chevrolet Corvettes, Ford Broncos, motorcycle rallies, and participants in the Richard Crane Memorial Truck Show, named for the founder of the American Truck Driving School in Coldwater, Michigan.

WALK THE MACKINAC BRIDGE

C'MON EVERYONE! HAVE FUN... WALKING 'MIGHTY MAC'

LABOR DAY MORNING

8:30 A.M.

North to South - 4 ½ Miles - Free

THE GREAT ANNUAL RECREATIONAL STROLL!

$1,000 in Prizes to Lucky Walkers!!

Also:

7:30 A.M. - Mich. A.A.U. Men & Boys Race Walks

7:45 A.M. - Mich. A.A.U. Women & Girls Race Walks

8:10 A.M. - I.W.A. Novice Race Walks

Medals - TROPHIES - Plaques

For Complete Information Write
MACKINAC BRIDGE AUTHORITY, ST. IGNACE, MICHIGAN

The poster advertising the first Mackinac Bridge Walk was really an invitation for participants in a speed-walking race. The numbers were small for that first event, held during the June 1958 dedication weekend. The numbers increased yearly, and from 1959, Labor Day Monday was chosen as the date to walk the bridge. In 1964, the direction was changed to begin in St. Ignace and finish in Mackinaw City, and it continued that way for more than 50 years. When 6,000 people showed up in 1964, organizers realized that the event had become something that consisted mostly of walkers from the Lower Peninsula who wanted to return home promptly after they finished. Today, walkers come from all across America and even foreign countries and can start and finish from either side.

Over the years, many participants returned from all over America and from countries around the world. They made the Mackinac Bridge Walk an annual event, proudly displaying patches that commemorated their feat. As the crowds grew, so did the number of unusual occurrences that had everyone talking on the way home. Some promoters, lobbyists, and protesters figured that it was pretty hard to pass up the chance to work a crowd of that size. Groups of all types and descriptions have walked the Mac over the years. Bands have played as they marched across. Veterans' groups have carried the flag in color guards that walked the five miles of the Mackinac Bridge Walk.

Gov. Jennifer Granholm enjoyed the Mackinac Bridge Walk and challenged herself to run across the five-mile span. She thought others would like it, too, and encouraged the Mackinac Bridge Authority to develop a "fun-run" race prior to the walking event. Granholm ran with her family or other children she invited to join in. For safety reasons, runners were selected by lottery from each of Michigan's 83 counties and several state agencies to enjoy the honor, restricting the number who could run with Granholm to around 300. There was never a shortage of applicants from anywhere in the state. The runners line up before sunrise and complete the route before the walk begins.

Runners complete their journey across the Mackinac Bridge in varying finish times but are always across before the walkers thanks to their head start. The normal crossing time for "casual" walkers is about two hours. In 1969, Michigan governor William G. Milliken accompanied a crowd of 16,000 who walked the bridge—and many wanted to share the experience with the new governor. The picture-taking and hand-shaking slowed the "speed-walking" governor down to a 51-minute crossing. It was not until 1970 that Milliken clocked an elapsed time of 46 minutes and 50 seconds, a record that stood for many years as the fastest gubernatorial crossing and is still the fastest that any governor has "walked" across the bridge. Milliken did so among a crowd of more than 20,000 walkers that year.

Not everyone can walk or run across the Mackinac Bridge on Labor Day, but that does not mean those with disabilities cannot participate. An amazing number of bridge-crossers do so in wheelchairs, and many really move across quickly. In 1994, fourteen people from an organ transplant group showed up to prove their good health. Among their members were those who had had a heart transplant, a liver transplant, and a woman who said she was the recipient of the first-ever double lung transplant. They all made it across. Some laid claim to the fact that they had walked the bridge every year the event had been held. Others would sometimes walk the span, hop on the bus ride back over to St. Ignace, and do it again.

Different Michigan governors have put their own stamp on the way they crossed the bridge. Gov. James Blanchard, a smiling personality who attracted crowds everywhere he went, was in no hurry and walked while carrying on conversations with those around him. Thousands would drive home and tell their friends that they had walked the bridge with Jim Blanchard, and they would be correct.

Gov. John Engler casually pushed a stroller across with his triplet daughters aboard. He was accompanied by the most visible security force for any governor on a Mackinac Bridge Walk in 50 years. Gov. Jennifer Granholm, a runner who encouraged fitness among Michigan citizens, took off and ran across the bridge in 2003, her first year in office, and beat all previous crossing times by past governors. She was joined by her family on several occasions.

The crowds increased steadily until 1992 when an unprecedented visitor arrived to walk the Mackinac Bridge—the president of the United States. Pres. George H.W. Bush led an array of local political leaders, gawkers, and Secret Service agents across that day. His long strides kept him well ahead of the estimated crowd of 85,000 that also crossed, an all-time record. Gov. Rick Snyder (above) was a walker and was usually joined by family members and Lt. Gov. Brian Calley. Gov. Gretchen Whitmer (below) walked at a pretty good pace, took an occasional jog, and made time to talk to bridge-crossers during her terms as Michigan's governor.

The Mackinac Bridge Walk is made possible each Labor Day by the cooperative effort of local law enforcement agencies and the Michigan State Police. The Michigan National Guard continues security on the actual bridge span. Lost children are reunited with their parents, directions are given to walkers to help find parked automobiles, and first aid and water are administered to those in need. The United States Coast Guard patrols the waters below along with sheriff's department boats. A massive army of local volunteers in Mackinaw City and St. Ignace are also on the job from 4:00 a.m. until well past noon to make it all happen. After President Bush's 1992 walk set the record, subsequent attendance numbers dropped to the normal established range of 50,000–60,000, where they remained until the COVID-19 pandemic that canceled the 2020 event. Facing numerous challenges, numbers have slowly increased, and the bridge walk is still the world's greatest walking event, becoming a unique Michigan tradition.

As more participants arrived, the logistics of the event became an issue, with transportation of the walkers becoming impossible with just the two buses owned by the Mackinac Bridge Authority. They needed a ride from one side of the bridge to the other—before or after the walk. In 1983, the numbers were up to 43,000 walkers, and 70 area school buses were commissioned from throughout Northern Michigan, one day before most schools began classes. By then, the plan had been perfected, with walkers from either side riding a bus across from Mackinaw City to St. Ignace and walking from St. Ignace to Mackinaw City. The order in which they did so depended on their starting and finishing points. The number of buses needed rose to more than 125 by the early 1990s. The charge was just $5, a bargain for the day's entertainment.

By 2018, world events made the potential for a terrorist act during the bridge walk both painfully obvious and horrifying. After first closing the bridge to all traffic except the school buses during the event, officials decided in later years to ban all vehicles. The initial public response was negative, but eventually, the process smoothed out through communication and media coverage.

The bridge is closed on Labor Day Monday from 6:30 a.m. until noon. Participants can now walk as much—or as little—as they want before turning back. They can also walk the entire five-mile length, or start early enough and walk all the way over and back. Then they can claim to be a "double-crosser."

Comparing these two images taken from aloft shows the relative difference between the era when vehicles were permitted on the Mackinac Bridge during the bridge walk and modern times when only pedestrians were allowed. Safety has always been the top priority during this event and the risks of large vehicles driving into crowds of people became too great, intentional or not. The policy of "pedestrians only" on the bridge that followed the COVID-19 pandemic has been refined to perfection and is so simple that the public has embraced it. Motorists have to plan their travels to account for the closure until noon, but even that can be dealt with in advance. Police, fire, and medical personnel plan their procedures accordingly, and ferryboats offer alternate crossings that morning if needed.

The Mackinac Bridge Authority is pleased to host various parade groups and strives to allow the events to take place in a safe, organized atmosphere. A permit is necessary in advance to secure permission to cross the bridge in this manner. The Corvette Crossroads adds a classy salute to its program by parading across the Mackinac Bridge. The event is held in Mackinaw City in August and draws plenty of attention with its evening crossing, held with usually cooperative warm weather and convertible tops down. The Mustang Stampede is also in August and is well attended with a variety of models representing many years of production. Both events feature social activities, awards ceremonies, and merchandise expos. (Courtesy of James Tamlyn.)

The Jeeps get their parade too, seen here lining up on Interstate 75 to cross the bridge in early May from St. Ignace to Mackinaw City. Unique in their design and their ownership, Jeeps have their own identity being built in Toledo, Ohio. Jeep the Mac is an event organized by the St. Ignace Visitors Bureau. It takes place in St. Ignace and via ferry to Drummond Island and includes trail riding and mudbogging. Not to be outdone, Ford Broncos have also paraded across the bridge in large numbers. Vendors often sell apparel and merchandise relating to their brand. (Courtesy of the St. Ignace Visitors Bureau.)

In terms of sheer numbers, it is hard to beat the massive assemblage of MINI Coopers shown in this aerial photograph from above the Little Bear East Arena parking lot. More than 1,300 MINI Coopers gathered for MINI on the Mack, held in early August and organized by MINI of Grand Rapids with support from MINI USA. In 2023, the group gathered to try and break the English-held world record for the largest-ever MINI Cooper parade, at 1,450 vehicles. The event raised more than $31,000 for the Van Andel Institute Purple Community, a charity that helps advance research for Parkinson's disease. (Courtesy of the St. Ignace Visitors Bureau.)

The Mackinac Bridge Antique Tractor Crossing has been a favorite for participants and spectators alike since it began in 2008. The only day of the year when one can legally drive a farm tractor across the bridge, the event is held one week after Labor Day and is limited to the first 1,500 tractors that are at least 40 years old and meet other requirements. Organized by Owosso Tractor Parts, the parade has seen tractors from as far away as Arizona and New York, with about half of the United States represented and an abundance of American flags flying.

Participants have also come from Canada, Texas, Florida, and California. Tractors show up in all colors—green, red, blue, white, yellow, and even pink. Rust is regarded as a color, too. Trek the Mighty Mac is a parade event for all-terrain or off-road vehicles, including ATVs, side-by-sides, and off-road motorcycles. Held in late September/early October, the parade has been called a rolling exhibit of off-road machinery, old and new.

For years, cycling events and bicycle crossings, including the Big Mac Shoreline Spring and Fall Scenic Tours, were sponsored by cycling groups, usually taking place at 6:00 a.m. and restricted to riders aged 13 years and older. After traveling a choice of several different routes leading to Mackinaw City, the cyclists would join locals in pedaling across the bridge and back, along with vehicular bridge traffic. The bike parades on the bridge ended when the Mackinac Bridge Authority deemed the event too dangerous to conduct with traffic alongside. The possibilities of tragedy became too great when coupled with increasing driver distraction, vehicle speed, and bicycle group control issues. The only parade event with enough participants to close the bridge to vehicular traffic today remains the bridge walk. Running events were also affected and are now restricted to Labor Day. (Courtesy of the Mackinaw Area Visitors Bureau.)

The line of lighted, decorative trucks in the Richard Crane Memorial Truck Show draws crowds from downtown St. Ignace to the Mackinac Bridge approach to downtown Mackinaw City. The truck show is a most unusual sight, with more than 100 trucks participating in the Mackinac Bridge Parade of Lights. The Michigan Department of Transportation gives annual permission for the trucks to display all their lights in the parade. The trucks are decorated with trim lights, underside lighting, black lighting, and moving images and murals that cast an eerie, other-worldly glow upon the bridge. Most lean on their horns for much of the journey, providing perhaps the loudest parade by far.

The Mackinac Bridge Authority is accustomed to providing transports for snowmobiles across the bridge by using a flatbed trailer that can haul eight sleds per trip. But the most recent addition to the bridge's parade line up is Snowmobile the Mighty Mac, organized by the Top of the Lake Snowmobile Club in conjunction with the St. Ignace Visitors Bureau. Held in early December, the event includes antique and vintage snowmobiles equipped with front-wheel kits. The sleds must have a minimum of two-inch-wide wheels and no studs or cleats. Drivers must be at least 12 years old with a youth snowmobile safety class certificate. Participants must be able to drive across the bridge under their own power, but a trailer is available to assist any sled that develops a problem and cannot complete the crossing. All bridge parades are subject to the Mackinac Bridge Authority's construction and maintenance schedules. (Courtesy of the St. Ignace Visitors Bureau.)

Eight

SUPREME SACRIFICES

The construction industry has undergone many changes over the years, due in large part to OSHA regulations and the advent of modern safety equipment, engineering, and architectural designs. But in the early 1950s, estimates of one life being lost for every $10 million spent added up to nearly a dozen fatalities predicted to occur during construction. In fact, the lives of five workmen were lost while the bridge was being built between 1954 and 1957. Another died during maintenance work in 1997.

Each a heartbreaking tragedy, the number was far below what was predicted by the "rule of thumb" forecast by those in the industry, making the building and day-to-day work performed on the Mighty Mac quite safe in retrospect.

On the day the bridge was dedicated, June 28, 1958, the Michigan Building and Trades Council dedicated two bronze plaques, one engraved with the names of the five men who died during the construction of the Mackinac Bridge and the other with the dignitaries responsible for financing and organizing the project. They were located on the west side of Pier 1. On July 29, 1999, the plaques were rededicated and moved to the pillar closest to the entrance of the Colonial Michilimackinac Visitor's Center to be more visible to the public. During the bridge's 50th anniversary celebration in 2007, a statue of a bridge worker was erected in Bridgeview Park to honor those who died during construction. The Mackinac Bridge Authority named the street between the maintenance garage and the office building Daniel Doyle Drive in memory of the maintenance worker who died in 1997.

The beginning stages of the first construction season, 1954, did not start well when three lives were lost in separate accidents during a 45-day period. Hard-hat diver Frank Pepper became the first bridge fatality at the Straits of Mackinac on September 10, 1954. An experienced diver with more than 20 years of underwater work, Pepper had been working for Merritt-Chapman & Scott at a depth of 140 to 150 feet for nearly an hour inspecting Pier 19, the bridge's south tower. Tired and cold, Pepper signaled to his tender that he wanted to come up immediately. Somehow in the process, the diver was either raised too quickly or himself prompted too speedy an ascent but upon surfacing was discovered to have contracted "the bends," or decompression sickness. Pepper was taken to a recompression chamber to attempt to dissolve the nitrogen bubbles that had formed in his bloodstream. He died before a doctor arrived.

Another Merritt-Chapman & Scott employee was lost exactly one month later on October 10, 1954, when James R. LeSarge, 26 years old, was killed in a fall inside the reinforced steel caisson foundation of Pier 20, the bridge's north tower. A welder working on cross sections of reinforcement pieces within the caisson, LeSarge fell through several steel braces and hit his head. He then underwent a 40-foot drop to the bottom of the caisson, which was being filled with concrete. Stories often circulate about a worker who is buried in the Mackinac Bridge, but according to those who were on the job they are not true. It is believed that LeSarge died before reaching the bottom of the foundation. Very little of the surface area of the concrete pour was actually wet due to the rapid formation of the concrete already in place underneath. His body was immediately recovered.

Only 15 days later, a local laborer from St. Ignace drowned, creating very low morale among the work crews. These men were wearing heavy clothing, tool belts, and work boots—certainly not dressed to swim. Albert B. Abbott slipped and fell into the Straits of Mackinac while walking on a beam from his workboat to his workstation toward Mackinaw City. The beam was 18 inches wide and only four feet above the water where he was working on a bridge foundation. He did not surface, causing his coworkers to jump in after him, but he was not immediately found. He was dead by the time his body was recovered, and it was later learned that Abbott had suffered a heart attack.

The next two workers died on June 6, 1956, after falling from near the top of the north tower. Jack C. Baker, a 28-year-old from Pagosa Springs, Colorado, and 27-year-old Robert Koppen of Plymouth, Michigan, were working their first day on the job for the American Bridge Division when the accident occurred.

These men were installing chain-link fence to create a spinners' platform. This is an area where the cable spinners could work while handling the thin wires that would be bulked together to comprise the main cables that support the bridge. Bundles of the chain-link fence, folded up like road maps, were to be raised to the top of each tower. Five heavier wire ropes had been stretched from anchor block to anchor block, the complete 8,614 foot length of the total suspension. The bundles were tied to the wire ropes with U-shaped brackets so they could slide down the wire ropes as they were unfolded. To hold the packages in place, a restraining line was tied to control their speed and the rate of descent down the supporting ropes.

There was no roadway below yet, only open air above the water as the construction crews worked to link the bridge towers and anchor piers with cable. Robert Anderson, in charge of the detail, and his assistant Louis Stepman stood at the top of the tower to push each package with their feet to allow gravity to help the chain-link fence segments unfold. Suddenly, the restraining line snapped. The 100-foot package of fencing and supporting 8-by-10-inch, 10-foot wooden ties slid out of control down the wire ropes and caught Jack Baker and Robert Koppen wrapped up inside, dooming them to plunge into the Straits of Mackinac from a height of more than 500 feet. Stepman and Anderson fell when the bundle crashed but grabbed the fence and held on for their lives. Baker's body did not sink and was soon recovered, but there was no sign of Koppen. Work on the bridge was suspended while a three-day search commenced with boats and divers, but Koppen was never found.

Mackinac Bridge workers went on the job every day and brought a lunch bucket and a lot of grit. Working in often uncomfortable weather conditions, safety was always a priority for these men. The extreme heights, the forbidding depths of the water below them, and the physical demands of their work tested the fortitude of the workmen. However, they kept at it and completed the bridge on time and on budget. The deaths that did occur were all tragedies but were far less than what had been predicted for a project of this magnitude.

The Mackinac Bridge claimed one of its own on August 7, 1997, when a bridge maintenance worker fell from a scaffold 70 feet into the Straits of Mackinac and drowned. Daniel Doyle, 42 years old, of Sault Ste. Marie was working with another painter on a 40-foot-long swing platform, or "pick," a motorized scaffold similar to those used by high-rise window washers. Doyle, a steeplejack with the bridge's maintenance crew for 12 years, fell while painting within box beams on the underside of the bridge just north of the south anchor pier, known as Pier 17. The Mackinac Bridge Authority's boat arrived within several minutes but could not find Doyle. His body was eventually recovered. The street leading to the maintenance building was named for Daniel Doyle, and the Mackinac Bridge Authority's boat is now always in the water near anywhere work is being done.

During the 2007 celebration of the Mackinac Bridge's 50th anniversary, a statue was unveiled at Bridgeview Park depicting an ironworker crossing on a beam four feet high, honoring Albert Abbott, who died falling into the Straits of Mackinac in exactly that circumstance. The call had been issued for bridge workers' clothing of a particular size and tools donated to be used for the statue. Everything from the helmet, clothing, and tool belt down to the shoes worn by various bridge workers were dressed upon the form, then bronzed and placed on the beam in the park. The names of the five men who died are inscribed on a plaque affixed to the base to honor them all.

Nine

SEPTEMBER 22, 1989, AND MARCH 2, 1997

In the Mackinac Bridge's history, two dates stand out as the most public of all since it opened—dates that combined terror, tragedy, grief, and controversy. The first date is September 22, 1989, when a light blue 1987 Yugo driven by Leslie Ann Pluhar of Royal Oak, Michigan, went off the Mackinac Bridge. A young woman's life ended in unimaginable horror, dying in perhaps the most spectacular way possible in Michigan, falling in a car from the state's most celebrated structure—its very symbol since 1957. A family wrestled with incomprehensible grief for eight days until her body was recovered. Claims that the bridge was unsafe resulted in a lawsuit, settled out of court five years later. The tragedy caused many who had crossed the bridge at one time or another to ponder the sheer terror of the accident. At 6:40 p.m. that Friday night, witnesses said the car careened out of control about 600 feet north of the bridge's south tower, struck the center median, straddled it for about 70 feet, and then swerved back across two lanes and hit an 11-inch-high curb rail almost head-on, flipping up along a railing three feet, two inches high and skidding for almost 40 feet, clipping off a streetlight pole before spinning sideways and hitting a vertical suspender cable. The car then fell—possibly upside down—onto a 21-inch girder that slopes down at a 45-degree slant for about 40 feet, where it meets a vertical and a horizontal girder. Then the car plunged into the water, dropping free and clear for 180 feet and likely reaching 70 miles per hour by impact. The medical examiner's autopsy report listed blunt force trauma and drowning as the cause of Pluhar's death.

On March 2, 1997, a southbound 1996 dark green Ford Bronco driven at high speed by 25-year-old Richard Alan Daraban passed a slow-moving tractor trailer at mid-span and suddenly swerved hard to the right, skidded along the bridge rail, and pitched over the side, falling 200 feet into the Straits of Mackinac. State police determined that Daraban had driven off the bridge deliberately.

Leslie Ann Pluhar, 31 years old, was traveling north to visit her boyfriend, 34-year-old Frederick Burton of Gould City, Michigan, about 50 miles northwest of St. Ignace, when she had an accident that caused her car to plummet over the side of the Mackinac Bridge in the approximate location pictured here. Her driving record was cited by some as proof that the accident was likely caused by driver error. She had four speeding convictions, one drunken driving conviction, two license suspensions, and one restriction between 1982 and 1984. She had not received any tickets since her license had been reinstated in February 1985.

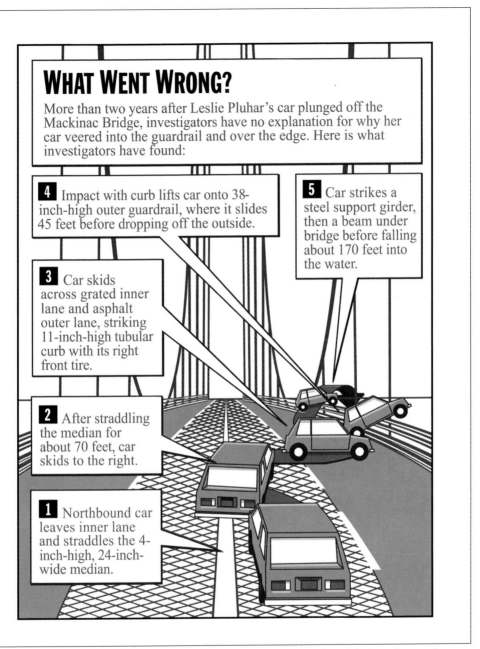

WHAT WENT WRONG?

More than two years after Leslie Pluhar's car plunged off the Mackinac Bridge, investigators have no explanation for why her car veered into the guardrail and over the edge. Here is what investigators have found:

4 Impact with curb lifts car onto 38-inch-high outer guardrail, where it slides 45 feet before dropping off the outside.

5 Car strikes a steel support girder, then a beam under bridge before falling about 170 feet into the water.

3 Car skids across grated inner lane and asphalt outer lane, striking 11-inch-high tubular curb with its right front tire.

2 After straddling the median for about 70 feet, car skids to the right.

1 Northbound car leaves inner lane and straddles the 4-inch-high, 24-inch-wide median.

Michigan State Police investigators estimated Leslie Pluhar's speed at 55–63 miles per hour, a factor they said helped make the nearly head-on collision with the curb rail so deadly. Eyewitnesses contended that strong winds helped push the car off the bridge. But a wind gauge at the center span, which would have recorded higher speeds than at the accident scene 600 feet north of the south tower, only clocked steady 35-mile-per-hour winds during the hour before and after the accident with a maximum gust of 48 miles per hour. Later that night, substantially windier conditions prevailed as the storm increased in intensity. The temperature at 7:00 p.m. on the evening of the tragedy was 43 degrees, and the road deck was mostly dry, though rain fell in the area earlier. (Courtesy of the *Detroit News*.)

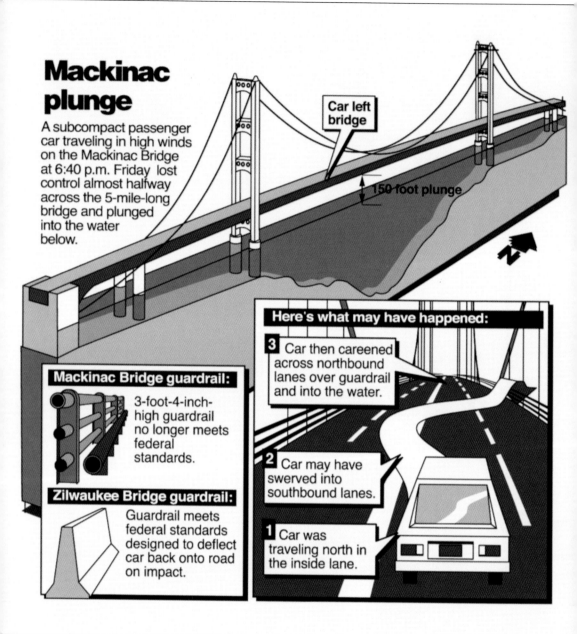

Mackinac plunge

A subcompact passenger car traveling in high winds on the Mackinac Bridge at 6:40 p.m. Friday lost control almost halfway across the 5-mile-long bridge and plunged into the water below.

Car left bridge

↕ 150-foot plunge

Mackinac Bridge guardrail:

3-foot-4-inch-high guardrail no longer meets federal standards.

Zilwaukee Bridge guardrail:

Guardrail meets federal standards designed to deflect car back onto road on impact.

Here's what may have happened:

3 Car then careened across northbound lanes over guardrail and into the water.

2 Car may have swerved into southbound lanes.

1 Car was traveling north in the inside lane.

Witnesses and media accounts varied as to how the accident might have occurred. "I think she had five, maybe six seconds before she hit the water," said Max Coburn, the Mackinac Bridge Authority's chief engineer, after studying the accident scene. "The car was going at a high rate of speed and she hit the brakes on the steel grating lane, then let up on the brakes, hit the rail and bounced up, hit the other rail and kept on sliding, and rolled over the rail," Coburn theorized. Trucker Donald Klassen of Manitoba was driving his rig on the outside lane, about five car lengths behind the Yugo, which had just passed him. He did not think Pluhar tried to stop. "Even when she crossed the median, her brake lights did not come on," he told the *Detroit Free Press*. (Courtesy of the *Detroit News*.)

Bridge tragedy

After examining physical evidence on the Mackinac Bridge, authorities say this is what happened Friday night when Leslie Pluhar's small car sailed off the bridge:

Blue Yugo begins to swerve out of control. Witnesses said wind gusts caused the car to go out of control and said the car was obeying the 45 mph speed limit. Bridge authorities believe excessive speed by the driver is to blame.

Car swerves into the southbound lanes before swerving back into the northbound lanes.
Skid marks were found on the grating and on the asphalt outside lane.

Car slams nearly head-on into curb railing, tilts to one side and slides along the outer railing for about 40 feet.

Car spins sideways and hits a vertical suspension cable and slides down along a 40 ft. girder.

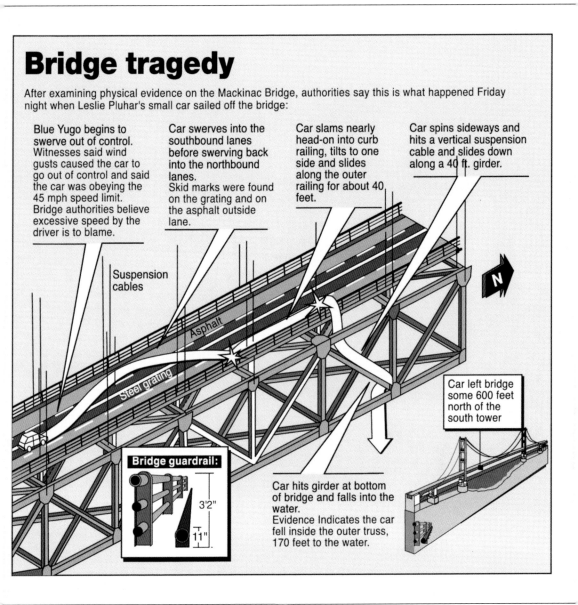

Suspension cables

Asphalt

Steel grating

N

Bridge guardrail:

3'2"

11"

Car left bridge some 600 feet north of the south tower

Car hits girder at bottom of bridge and falls into the water.
Evidence Indicates the car fell inside the outer truss, 170 feet to the water.

The story of the Yugo was far from over, proven by a $2 million lawsuit filed by the Pluhar family that contended the bridge had inadequate warnings for bad weather, substandard guardrails, an insufficient dividing strip, and dangerous gratings in the middle lanes of the suspended portion of the span. Eventually, the New York engineering firm of Steinman, Boynton, Gronquist, and Birdsall, which built the bridge, settled their share with the family for $50,000. Anthony Motors, the dealer that sold Pluhar the Yugo, paid the family the vehicle's cost of $5,000. After reports that Aetna Insurance, representing the Mackinac Bridge Authority and the Michigan Department of Transportation, had offered the family $350,000–with the family reportedly still asking for $800,000–the two sides settled in Macomb County Circuit Court on September 16, 1994, at $500,000 through the aid of a mediation panel of three lawyers. (Courtesy of the *Detroit News*.)

Less than eight years later, a Ford Bronco rammed the railing at the bridge's center span and flipped over the side, breaking through the ice below and sinking to the bottom of the Straits of Mackinac. Witnesses stated that Richard Daraban was traveling at a high rate of speed, estimated by Michigan State Police who measured "yaw marks" from the vehicle's tires on the bridge railing at 60–65 miles per hour. Police added that there was no evidence that Daraban tried to stop the car, and an eyewitness said the 1997 incident appeared to be deliberate. Daraban's body was thrown clear of the vehicle and recovered from the ice surface. As of 2024, less than two dozen people have taken their own lives from the Mackinac Bridge. (Left, courtesy of Terry Fitzpatrick; below, courtesy of the *Detroit Free Press*.)

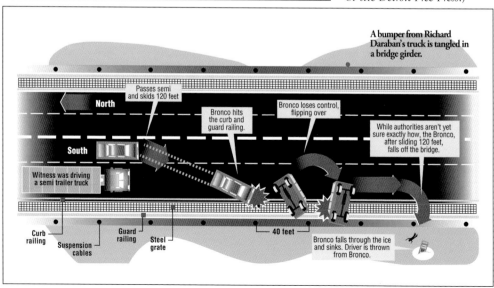

A bumper from Richard Daraban's truck is tangled in a bridge girder.

North

Passes semi and skids 120 feet

Bronco hits the curb and guard railing.

Bronco loses control, flipping over

While authorities aren't yet sure exactly how, the Bronco, after sliding 120 feet, falls off the bridge.

South

Witness was driving a semi trailer truck

Curb railing

Suspension cables

Guard railing

Steel grate

40 feet

Bronco falls through the ice and sinks. Driver is thrown from Bronco.

Ten

"IF YOU SEEK A PLEASANT PENINSULA, LOOK ABOUT YOU"

In 1999, the Mackinac Bridge was selected as the state's No. 1 civil engineering project of the 20th century by the Michigan Section of the American Society of Civil Engineers (ASCE). An average of 12,000 vehicles cross the Mackinac Bridge per day, with full traffic loads of 60,000 vehicles estimated during holiday periods. Ship traffic under the bridge is responsible for millions of tons of iron ore annually freighted to steel mills along with other cargoes to various ports. Nearly 40,000 vehicles have crossed the bridge in one 24-hour period—during a weekend of the St. Ignace Antique Auto Show—a one-day record.

Expertly maintained, fully funded, and amazingly resilient to the many forces and factors of man and nature that have failed to seriously affect its status as the lone highway link between Michigan's two main peninsulas, the Mighty Mac has endured plenty. The structure is ready for more—lots more. The bridge is perhaps the most photographed feature among the state's icons and has as many faces and moods as there are angles of sun, moon, and weather. People drive from long distances to see it and enjoy the clean water-washed air of the Straits Area and its beaches, forests, and attractions.

The Mackinac Bridge Authority hosted a grand opening of its new $1.3 million eight-acre Bridge View Park on June 12, 2002. It is a beautiful setting for the public to experience a spectacular view of the Mackinac Bridge and the Straits Area. The new park includes paved access roads, a walking path, picnic areas, trees, and landscaped areas containing flowers and shrubs. On the Mackinaw City side, public parks line the shores near the Old Mackinac Point Lighthouse, giving access to the water and a fabulous view of the bridge from the south. Seasonal restroom facilities are available with sidewalks, drinking fountains, and picnic areas. Truly, the Straits of Mackinac epitomizes the state motto of Michigan, "Si quaeris peninsulam amoenam, circumspice," or "If you seek a pleasant peninsula, look about you."

The Golden Gate Bridge only cost $36 million to build in 1937. But David Steinman knew that he faced challenges far different from those seen in San Francisco Bay. In the Straits of Mackinac, the winds and waves would be worse, and the water would freeze into ice that could be 10 feet thick during buildups that threatened to sweep clear anything left on the surface. Steinman also had to factor in that the suspended span of the Mackinac Bridge would be longer than that of the Golden Gate Bridge.

Another situation that David Steinman resolved to avoid was that of the Tacoma Narrows Bridge disaster. Situated on the Tacoma Narrows in Puget Sound, near the city of Tacoma, Washington, the bridge had only been open for traffic for a few months when trouble occurred. On November 7, 1940, at approximately 11:00 a.m., the first Tacoma Narrows suspension bridge collapsed due to wind-induced vibrations. Steinman's design was built to withstand far more wind than had destroyed the Tacoma Narrows Bridge, ensuring that a disaster like the one that occurred there would never take place at the Straits of Mackinac.

As of 2023, there have been several proposals and several weddings on the Mackinac Bridge. There have also been three babies born on the bridge. Shawn Shuman arrived on May 11, 1983, to Kim Shuman in a Kinross Township ambulance that stopped at Pier 17, the south anchor pier. Anastasia Marie Johnson was delivered in an ambulance that was crossing the bridge on May 24, 1997. Her mother, Yvette Johnson, gave birth to her fourth daughter a short time after winning $60 at the slot machines at the Kewadin Shores Casino in St. Ignace. Due to HIPAA regulations, little is known about a third birth that bridge officials say took place in the early 2000s in a car while crossing at mid-span.

Bridge parades, milestone crossings, tollbooth tales, historic moments, and tragedies are all part of the Mackinac Bridge's history. Those who have crossed it all seem to have a story to tell, even those in the majority that were uneventful. Those who maintain it, collect tolls, or work in operations do so with a fierce personal pride, a sense of teamwork, and a successful track record in their caretaking of the Mighty Mac. Because of them, Dr. David B. Steinman's miracle design continues to stand as a proud icon of the state of Michigan. (Courtesy of the Mackinaw Area Visitors Bureau.)

DISCOVER THOUSANDS OF LOCAL HISTORY BOOKS FEATURING MILLIONS OF VINTAGE IMAGES

Arcadia Publishing, the leading local history publisher in the United States, is committed to making history accessible and meaningful through publishing books that celebrate and preserve the heritage of America's people and places.

Find more books like this at
www.arcadiapublishing.com

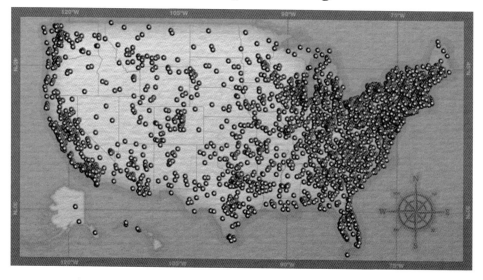

Search for your hometown history, your old stomping grounds, and even your favorite sports team.

Consistent with our mission to preserve history on a local level, this book was printed in South Carolina on American-made paper and manufactured entirely in the United States. Products carrying the accredited Forest Stewardship Council (FSC) label are printed on 100 percent FSC-certified paper.

MADE IN THE USA